Modelling and predicting property crime trends

in England and Wales

by
Sanjay Dhiri,
Sam Brand,
Richard Harries and
Richard Price

A Research, Development and Statistics Directorate Report

London: Home Office

Home Office Research Studies

The Home Office Research Studies are reports on research undertaken by or on behalf of the Home Office. They cover the range of subjects for which the Home Secretary has responsibility. Titles in the series are listed at the back of this report (copies are available from the address on the back cover). Other publications produced by the Research, Development and Statistics Directorate include Research Findings, the Research Bulletin, Statistical Bulletins and Statistical Papers.

The Research, Development and Statistics Directorate

 RDS is part of the Home Office. The Home Office's purpose is to build a safe, just and tolerant society in which the rights and responsibilities of individuals, families and communities are properly balanced and the protection and security of the public are maintained.

RDS is also a part of the Government Statistical Service (GSS). One of the GSS aims is to inform Parliament and the citizen about the state of the nation and provide a window on the work and performance of government, allowing the impact of government policies and actions to be assessed.

Therefore -

Research Development and Statistics Directorate exists to improve policy making, decision taking and practice in support of the Home Office purpose and aims, to provide the public and Parliament with information necessary for informed debate and to publish information for future use.

First published 1999
Application for reproduction should be made to the Information and Publications Group, Room 201, Home Office, 50 Queen Anne's Gate, London SW1H 9AT.

Foreword

In 1998 the Home Office developed two models of property crime, based on long-run aggregate relationships between recorded crime and macroeconomic and demographic factors. These have been updated and revised to incorporate new techniques and, for the first time, to investigate the implications of projecting trends in crime on the basis of the macro-level relationships captured by the econometric model. The resulting three-year projections help us to form broad judgements about the likely strength of underlying pressures on the level of property crime.

Though an understanding of possible future pressures on crime is important for planning in the criminal justice system and for other crime reduction measures, very little work has been undertaken in this field. By publishing these projections, we hope to stimulate debate about the use and possible extension of such models. In this spirit we would very much welcome comments on this report.

Richard Harries
Economics and Resources Analysis Unit
Home Office
November 1999

If you would like to comment on this paper, please contact:
Richard Harries,
Home Office RDS Economics & Resource Analysis Unit,
Room 266,
50 Queen Anne's Gate,
London SW1H 9AT,
United Kingdom.

Tel   +44 (0)20 7273 4030
Fax   +44 (0)20 7273 4013
E-mail Richard.Harries@HomeOffice.gsi.gov.uk

Acknowledgements

This paper would not have been possible without the earlier work by Simon Field.

It is fair to say that our analysis has generated a lively debate within the Home Office, and we would like to thank in particular Carole Willis for her incisive observations, and Pat Mayhew and Peter Goldblatt for their comments on earlier drafts. Elsewhere in government, we are particularly grateful to Jonathan Ockenden and Najma Rajah from the Performance and Innovation Unit for their helpful comments.

We would like to thank Professors Cliff Attfield, Chris Hale and Ron Smith for their helpful remarks and insights on the methodology employed. Finally, we owe a debt of gratitude to our wives and partners who have suffered too many lonely evenings as we sought to draft and re-draft in pursuit of a final version. Any errors are, of course, our own.

Contents

Summary

Home Office research over the last decade attempted to model historical trends in the level of recorded property crime in England and Wales over the last half century. The research demonstrated that there has been a strong association between the level of recorded burglary and theft and some key economic and demographic factors. These factors could be used to model most of the changes in crime since the early 1950s and were interpreted as key underlying pressures on recorded property crime.

New Home Office work, reported in this paper, considers how far these historical relationships can be used to form a view of how property crime trends might develop in the future. This is important because, to ensure that anti-crime programmes are effective in combating crime, we need an understanding of the pressures they are likely to face over the next few years.

The models have therefore been updated and modified to try to project how trends in burglary and theft might change in the future. Projections based on these models suggest that strong upward pressures on property crime are emerging and that the sustained fall in recorded property crime over the last six years may be about to reverse. However, these projections need to be qualified by recent evidence that the relationship between the model predictors and trends in recorded property crime may be weakening.

The projections are not forecasts of future crime levels: they indicate the likely effects of economic and demographic changes on crime trends *assuming no other factors come into play.* In particular, they do not take into account any expected impact of crime reduction measures introduced by the Government. Nor do they suggest a mechanical linkage between crime and economic and demographic factors. *The models are not intended to give a full explanation of what causes crime* – that can be done only using micro-level causal analysis.

However, the models do improve our understanding of pressures on aggregate property crime trends at a macro level, and have proved reasonably reliable as a tool for projecting these. They are nevertheless subject to review, scrutiny and improvement. To that end we hope that this publication will prompt serious debate around the techniques used and the conclusions drawn.

1 Why model trends in crime?

The Home Office's econometric models of property crime are part of a developing analytical capability to support the Government's Crime Reduction Strategy – a wide-ranging group of measures for tackling crime and delivering the Government's targets.

The models – covering around two-thirds of all recorded crime in England and Wales – are designed to help us to understand the main pressures on the volume of crime at a macro-level and to give an indication of how the crime level might change in the future, reflecting these underlying pressures. This gives us a better understanding of what our programmes must be designed to achieve and helps to shape policies to get the biggest impact on crime as well as to develop and deliver our crime reduction targets.

As well as the models and projections based on them, the Home Office also makes use of strategic information derived from:

- appraisals of what impacts on crime our anti-crime programmes achieve, and new management arrangements to make sure that they deliver;

- new relationships with the police, prisons, probation based on new sets of efficiency and performance measures for these front-line agencies and for the wider Criminal Justice System;

- monitoring and evaluations both of existing policies and of measures being developed in the Crime Reduction Programme, which are giving us a better understanding of the micro-level drivers of crime and the comparative cost-effectiveness of options to prevent crime. These are helping to ensure that resources are devoted to policies that deliver the biggest possible sustained impact on crime.

When interpreting results from the models, it is important to understand what the models do not do. Firstly, *they do not predict the future level of property crime*. Instead, they estimate what changes in property crime patterns are likely to occur as a result of demographic and economic changes *assuming no other factors*, such as government policies to reduce crime, are at work. Its purpose is to alert Ministers to possible upward pressures on crime rates, and to allow them to adjust policies and programmes to respond in good time.

Secondly, *the models are not intended to give a full picture of what causes crime*. They are not designed to explain crime - that can only be done through disaggregate causal research. But they do allow us - by investigating macro-level relationships - to develop a broad understanding of the pressures on crime trends, and to predict how these pressures might influence trends in the future. The models have proved reasonably reliable as tools for doing this - though they are subject to continual review, external scrutiny and improvement. We hope this publication will promote a high quality debate around the techniques used and the conclusions drawn.

2 Previous research on trends in crime

Models relating crime with economic and demographic variables are not new. This paper draws on the work of Becker (1968), Field (1990), Pyle and Deadman (1994), Osborne (1995), Marvell and Moody (1996), Deadman and Pyle (1997), Hale (1997, 1998), Pudney *et al.* (1999), Steffensmeier and Harer (1999) and Witt *et al.* (1999). In particular, it is based upon earlier Home Office research by Field (1998) which attempted to model historical trends in the level of recorded crime in England and Wales over the last half century. The research focused on a subset of recorded property crime – burglary and theft and handling[1] – which accounts for around two-thirds of total recorded crime incidents (see Figure 1).

Figure 1: Composition of total recorded crime (1997)

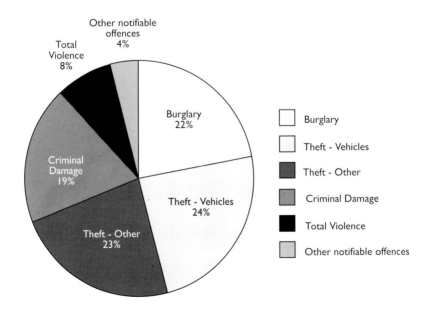

---

1   Excludes criminal damage. See Technical Annex for full data definitions.

3

Field was able to demonstrate a long-run cointegrating relationship between the economy, demographic factors and recorded burglary and theft. In the long-run, trends in thefts and burglaries were shown to be:

- linked to the stock of crime opportunities as measured by the stock of consumer goods. For every one per cent increase in this stock, burglary and theft increase by around two per cent; and

- associated with the number of young males. For every one per cent increase in the number of young males aged 15 and 20, burglary and theft increase by about one per cent.

Together, these factors were used in the model to determine an "equilibrium" or underlying level of property crime, which shifted over time reflecting changes in the two key variables (Figure 2). Field found that movements away from the underlying level tended to be corrected in subsequent years, so that any growth in actual recorded crime above the underlying level would be followed by downward pressure back to that underlying level.

Figure 2: Factors underlying the long-run level of burglary and theft

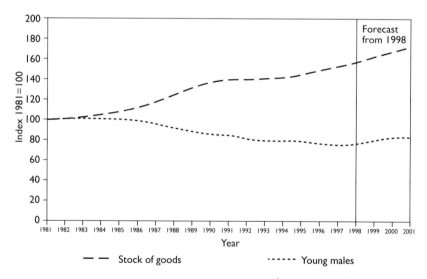

The models were able to account for most of the movement away from the underlying level, in the short-run, through the level of recorded burglary or theft in the previous year and changes in the annual growth rate of personal consumption. Rapid increases in consumer spending in a given year were associated with falling, or slower growth of, recorded property crime in that year. So there appeared to be a positive relationship between the growth in consumer spending and recorded property crime in the long-run but an inverse relationship in the short-run. Field described the former as an opportunity effect – more stealable goods in the economy – and the latter as a motivation effect – when people feel richer, as manifested by their spending, they are less likely to be attracted to criminal methods of obtaining goods.

3 How good have the models been?

There has been a good fit between changes in recorded property crime and changes expected on the basis of the models over the last 40 years, including the sustained fall in both burglary and theft from 1992 to 1996 (Figures 3 and 4). The fall of both burglary and theft can be viewed as a gradual return to the underlying level following the rapid rise between 1989 and 1992 – when recorded property crime increased by around 45 per cent in just three years.

Figure 3: Actual and modelled burglary and residuals 1952-1998

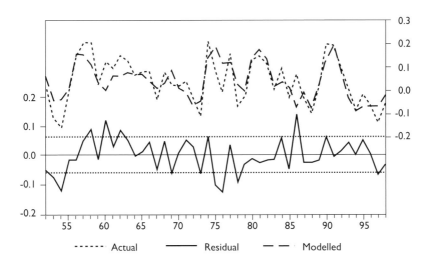

The burglary model has performed well in modelling trends throughout the entire period. Although the five per cent drop in burglaries in 1998 was unexpected on the basis of the model, the number of burglaries remains well within the 95 per cent confidence intervals for the model estimates.

The theft model on the other hand has been less successful in tracking changes in the level of crime in recent years. It failed to predict the extent of the fall in offences in 1997 – when the number of thefts fell by nine per cent

Figure 4: Actual and modelled theft and residuals 1952–1998

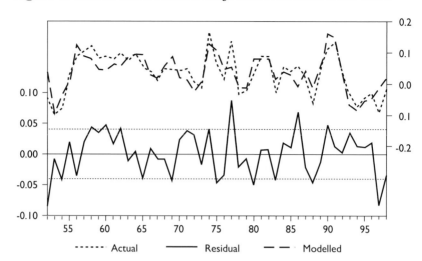

– and the continued, albeit more modest, fall in 1998. As a result the level of actual theft is now close to the lower bound of the 95 per cent confidence limits for the model estimates. Such divergence is not unprecedented. Since the theft model has provided a good fit for 40 years and even the unexpected fall did not push the level of recorded theft outside the confidence limits for the model estimates, it is too early to reject the model outright.

Nevertheless, this raises questions as to whether the relationships described by the model may be weakening. Formal tests to check for instability in the parameters in the theft model revealed that the theft model did indeed display some instability, not only in 1997 but also in the late 1960s and early 1970s. (These issues are investigated in detail in the Technical Annex.)

The earlier instability could be the result of changes to the recording rules for crime introduced in 1969, although the time series was adjusted to correct for these changes. It is possible that the theft and handling category was especially affected by the changes as it covers a more disparate group of offences. If this broad coverage is indeed behind this instability then the recent problems in the model could be explained by differences in trends between different types of theft offences.

Field pointed out that, although the models provide a good fit with historical trends, this should not be interpreted as a mechanical linkage between theft, burglary and the explanatory variables in the models. Any weakening of the models' explanatory power could be explained by a number of changes including:

- the introduction and adoption of better security systems and devices. New anti-crime measures to reduce specific crimes, expected to impact significantly on property crime, are not taken into account in the model. For example, the adoption of better security measures for vehicles and more secure parking would be expected to affect significantly the level of recorded crime;

- a stabilisation in the proportion of theft and burglary being reported to the police following the steep rise in reporting over the last two decades. The models are based on recorded, rather than actual, incidents of crime so that movements in recorded crime may reflect trends in reporting and recording practices rather than actual changes in the level of crime (Mirrlees-Black *et al.*, 1998);

- a shift away from theft and burglary to new types of acquisitive crime (e.g. computer fraud) which would not be categorised as theft and may be less well reported to the police;

- the impact of government policy aimed at reducing crime.

There is also international evidence that recorded crime is falling generally. Field found that some of the relationships that were observed in the UK could also be seen in the United States, though not elsewhere in Western Europe. In the USA the level of burglary and theft was closely linked to the "stock of crime opportunities" but Field also noted that there was a trend decline in recorded crime that was over and above any trends linked to economic factors.

4 Expanding the analysis

The results of the modelling exercise have to be interpreted carefully. Although the models have successfully explained most of the trends in the level of burglary and theft over the last 40 years, there are clearly many other factors that influence the level of burglary and theft that are not captured by these restricted national level models.

Policy variables

The models do not include any variables to measure the contribution of criminal policy. Consequently, they cannot be used to determine directly the effect of policy on crime levels. Instead the models provide an indication of the underlying economic and demographic pressures on property crime which may influence policy effectiveness. There are good reasons for excluding such variables.

Other studies that have tested the impact of policy variables at the national level have produced mixed results. Field (1990) analysed a wide range of variables, including police numbers and clear-up rates for a variety of crime categories. He found that, whilst clear-up rates were not significant, the number of police was negatively related to vehicle crime and other theft (though not to total theft). More recently, Witt *et. al.* (1999) found that police strength per capita was negatively correlated with property crime, particularly vehicle crime, whereas Beki *et. al.* (1999) reported a positive correlation between police numbers and a number of crimes (bicycle theft, violence against the person and criminal damage) in the Netherlands.

This confusion over the role of policy variables is confirmed by Marvell and Moody (1996), who report that, on the basis of 36 studies covering 78 crime regressions, 14 found significant negative coefficients on police variables whereas 17 found significant positive coefficients. The problem arises when researchers do not properly take into account the fact that criminal policy is generally formulated in the context of crime levels in preceding years. Marvell and Moody themselves found 'Granger-causality'[2] in both directions:

---

2   One variable is said to Granger-cause another if knowing past values of the first variable helps to explain current values of the second. This does not always accord with the more common understanding of causality. For example, higher consumer expenditure in November Granger-causes Christmas.

rising crime rates cause a small but highly significant increase in police levels, whereas higher police levels reduce most types of crime.

Unemployment

The many empirical studies of a causal link between unemployment and property crime provide mixed evidence and have been undertaken in many different ways. Two very recent and interesting examples are Hale (1997) and Witt *et. al.* (1999). Hale explored the impact on crime of the emergence of a dual-labour market – a secondary sector, characterised by part-time, low paid and intermittent employment, existing alongside the primary labour market. He found a long-run relationship between trends in recorded burglary and theft and the structure of employment. Witt *et al.* (1999) estimated a dynamic panel data model using aggregate data from 42 police force areas for the period 1986 to 1996. The research found a significant relationship between high property crime and both increases in male unemployment and high wage inequality.

5 Projecting future trends

Projecting changes in crime patterns on the basis of macroeconomic models is a complicated task. Forecasting is never an exact science as no single model can incorporate all causes of crime. Though there have been many studies to explain past trends in crime, few have attempted to make forecasts. However, the UK Government's focus on using evidence to shape policy in a more systematic way has made it more important to develop tools which give an indication of the pressures underlying both planning in the criminal justice system and wider policy initiatives to reduce crime.

Projections of both burglary and theft were made on the basis of the Home Office models. Although the models were not originally intended as tools for making projections, an extrapolation of past trends is still informative as it describes some of the underlying pressures on crime and, with careful interpretation, can provide a useful baseline for developing forecasts. The projections are based on official Treasury forecasts for the expected growth in household consumption and Government Actuary's Department (GAD) projections of the number of young men to 2001.

The strength of the economy in the mid-1990s and the associated rapid growth of consumer spending implies a high stock of consumer goods (crime opportunities) which will persist beyond 2001. Meanwhile GAD projections point to an increase in the number of young men in the next few years, reversing the steady fall since the early 1980s (Figure 2). These factors in combination add to the existing upward pressure on the level of recorded property crime, which was already well below the underlying level in 1998.

Short-run factors tell a mixed story. Treasury forecasts predict a stabilisation of the growth of household consumption between 1998 and 2001, below the average growth experienced in 1997 and 1998. But, since recorded crime has continued to fall in 1997 and 1998 and the rate of growth of crime appears to be strongly influenced by the previous year's growth rate, any expected growth in 1999 may well be suppressed.

Taking into account each of the long- and short-run factors, the models project a reversal of the sustained fall in both burglary and theft that has been observed over the last six years. The numbers of recorded burglaries and thefts are projected to increase substantially in the next three years (Figures 5 and 6).

Figure 5: Long-run model for burglary

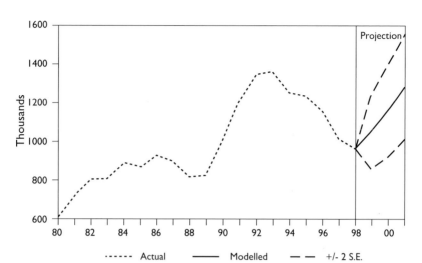

Figure 6: Long-run model for theft

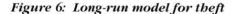

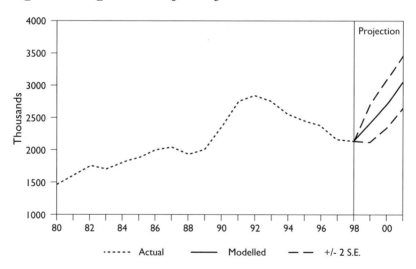

Theft and handling offences are projected to grow rapidly to over three million by 2001; around 40 per cent more than in 1997. The number of burglaries is also projected to increase but at a slower rate, rising to 1.3 million in 2001; a quarter more offences than in 1997.

There are wide margins of error around these projections. For thefts, though, even a lower range projection still indicates an annual average increase of at least five per cent a year. This would mean that recorded thefts would still rise by over 20 per cent between 1997 and 2001. The lower range projection for burglary shows that the number of recorded offences could even continue to fall in 1999 to below 900,000 for the first time in a decade, but would then start to rise. Even then the number of burglaries might still be marginally below the 1997 level in 2001.

Table 1:   Projections of burglary and theft 1997 – 2001

Year	Projected burglary (central projection)	95% confidence limits	Annual change	Change since 1997
	No. in millions	No. in millions	Percentage %	No. in millions
1997*	1.02			
1998*	0.97		-5	-0.1
1999	1.02	+/- 0.1	+6	0.0
2000	1.14	+/- 0.2	+11	+0.1
2001	1.28	+/- 0.3	+12	+0.3

Year	Projected theft (central projection)	95% confidence limits	Annual change	Change since 1997
	No. in millions	No. in millions	Percentage %	No. in millions
1997*	2.17			
1998*	2.14		-1	-0.1
1999	2.33	+/- 0.2	+9	+0.2
2000	2.65	+/- 0.3	+14	+0.5
2001	3.05	+/- 0.4	+15	+0.9

* actual crimes recorded

6 How reliable are the projections?

Projections based on extrapolating the models are only as robust as the models themselves. This suggests that while both models have generally performed well, we can be more certain about the burglary projections than those for theft. The projections also rely on the accuracy of forecasts for the independent economic and demographic variables.

A comprehensive review of the accuracy of Treasury forecasts by Melliss (1997) found that errors for consumers' expenditure were particularly bad in the late 1980s and early 1990s. The Treasury's own estimates, based on data for the preceding 10 years, suggest that the absolute average error for household consumption is $1/2$ per cent one year ahead and $1^1/4$ per cent two years ahead. A review of the accuracy of GAD projections by Shaw (1994) found that forecasts of the number of young males tend to be fairly accurate over a few years. The mean absolute error for five-year-ahead forecasts made between 1971 and 1987 of the population aged 15-19 was less than one per cent. Varying the forecasts of household consumption and the number of young males within these broad margins of error alters the projections of burglary and theft to 2001 only very slightly.

There remain several questions over the predictive power of the models. In particular, they do not take into account any expected impact of specific crime reduction measures introduced by the Government as well as other social and economic factors that could be expected to impact on property crime. *The projections should therefore be interpreted as describing underlying pressures on property crime based on historical trends and not as a prediction of the amount of future property crime.*

An illuminating test of the ability of the models to foresee changes in crime trends was carried out by re-estimating the models as if we were in 1988 and seeing whether projections based on the models accurately reflected trends in recorded property crime since then. Based only on information available in 1988, and assuming that economic and demographic forecasts made at the time were accurate, the burglary model would indeed have projected a sharp increase, although not the scale of the actual increase – recorded burglaries increased by 48 per cent between 1989 and 1991 (Figure 7).

Figure 7: Long-run model for burglary

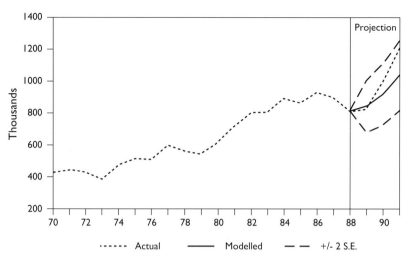

Note: Uncertainty surrounding crime trends means that projections beyond 3 years ahead are not reliable.

The theft model would also have correctly projected a significant increase (Figure 8).

Figure 8: Long-run model for theft

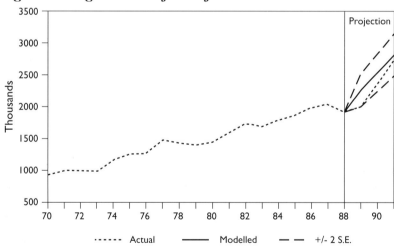

Note: Uncertainty surrounding crime trends means that projections beyond 3 years ahead are not reliable.

Of course the projections to 2001 are also only as good as the forecasts for the independent variables. They assume that the forecasts for the growth of household consumption in each of the next three years will be accurate. Any divergence from these forecasts will affect the crime projections.

7 Interpreting the projections

The projections produced by the model need very careful interpretation. Crime levels cannot be regarded as a mechanical product of economic and demographic variables. Indeed, interpretation is particularly difficult given that actual recorded theft in 1998 was at the lower confidence limit of model estimates.

How should we interpret this important departure of the outline data from the path predicted by the model? There are two principal, but not mutually exclusive, explanations:

- There has been a structural break in the theft model, and a lasting downward shift in the level of theft, for given levels of consumption and young males, has occurred. If this is true, we might expect to see a continued fall in crime, or small rises well below the projected levels.

- The model is still a good representation of the underlying relationship between theft and economic and demographic factors and 1997/1998 were unusual years characterised by historically low levels of recorded theft. But, as has happened in the past, theft is likely to return towards its equilibrium path with sharp rises in the next few years.

The recent behaviour of the economy (low inflation with low unemployment) may indicate that a structural break has occurred. However, for the moment and on balance, our judgement is that the latter explanation is the more likely. We know that the level of theft has departed substantially from the projected underlying rate in previous years, and has returned to it. However, this has not always happened quickly – the theft level remained within the confidence limits but above the model estimates for the six years from 1990.

Moreover, there is reason to think that 1998 may have been an unusual year. It marked the first major change to police counting rules for crime in 30 years. The figures in our dataset have been adjusted to take out the impact of these changes, although it is possible that, since the new counting rules took a while to bed down, we may need to re-visit this adjustment at some point in the future.

Our judgement is that, unless recent crime figures signal a departure from the long-running relationships expressed in the model, the level of theft will rise over the next few years as it moves back towards the underlying level. However, the rise may not be as rapid as the central projection would imply. We expect that, although the level of theft will remain within the lower bound of the projection to 2001, it may not rise as far as the central projection, since the return to the underlying level tends to happen only slowly, and theft is currently close to the lower bound. The level of theft will perhaps rise to midway between the lower and central projection, which suggests that theft would be around 30 per cent higher (650,000 more offences) than in 1997.

We have more confidence in the burglary model, which has continued to perform well in recent years. We expect burglary to remain close to the central projection, rising by around 26 per cent (250,000 offences) between 1997 and 2001. Overall, this suggests that in 2001 total recorded property crime would be some 30 per cent (900,000 offences) higher than in 1997, within a likely range of between 0.5 million and 1.4 million.

There are still unresolved questions over the validity of using the models to project crime levels, and further work will be done to try and improve their predictive power. The balance of evidence, however, clearly points to recorded burglary and theft rising by at least 17 per cent between 1997 and 2001, unless policy initiatives introduced in the last few years can constrain the substantial upward pressures. If the number of burglaries and thefts continues to fall for the next three years, this would represent a significant departure from a long-standing trend in recorded property crime.

8 Next steps

This paper suggests that trends in property crime can be projected using models based on the level of economic activity and demographic factors reflecting the number of young males in the age group with the highest propensity to commit crime. With some notable exceptions, relatively little attention has been devoted to this area in the past.

We intend to explore these issues further. In addition to a closer investigation of the impact on property crime of policy variables and unemployment, further modelling work is envisaged for other types of crime (eg. violent crime) and to test the application the model to other countries.[3] Similarly, where other factors appear to be significant elsewhere, these could be tested for the UK. A recent example is Steffensmeier and Harer (1999) who tested the relationship between crime and age distribution in the US (rather than numbers of young males), concluding that an ageing population is linked to falling crime.

In the development of these models several key issues have emerged for further research:

• a similar model of violent crime is already well developed and it is planned to investigate the feasibility of models for criminal damage, robbery and fraud and forgery;

• the relative weakness of the theft model suggests that there would be value in splitting it into a number of components - including vehicle crime;

• the relatively short run of annual data available (from 1951 onwards) is a constraint on this work. The use of quarterly data (available from the 1970s onward) provides an alternate approach. This would create a much larger dataset from which to draw inferences as well as allowing us to include variables that are not available over a longer time span (for example, income inequality and indicators of drug misuse);

---

3   Note, however, that the failure to replicate the England & Wales models in other countries does not mean that they
     are invalid for England and Wales.

- more sophisticated approaches to incorporation of changing patterns of crime reporting and other possible drivers of secular changes in recorded crime trends such as domestic insurance cover and home security;

- alternative approaches to incorporating demographic changes into the model – for example using measures of age dispersion rather than the number of young males;

- disaggregation to produce regional models may well also be worth investigating. This would allow a more sophisticated analysis of the impact of labour market changes and income inequality than has been possible at the aggregate, national level.

We encourage other researchers to consider what improvements could be made or alternative approaches adopted, and would welcome any comments on the models presented here and on the further work we propose.

References

Banerjee, A., Dolado, J., Galbraith, J. and Hendry, D. (1993). *Co-integration, Error-Correction, and the Econometric Analysis of Non-Stationary Data*, OUP, Oxford.

Becker, G. (1968). Crime and Punishment: An Economic Approach. *Journal of Political Economy*, 76: 169-217.

Beki, C., Zeelenberg, K. and Van Montfort, K. (1999). An analysis of the crime rate in the Netherlands 1950-93. *British Journal of Criminology*, 39: 401-415.

Deadman, D. and Pyle, D. (1997). Forecasting recorded property crime using a time-series econometric model. *British Journal of Criminology*, 37: 437-445.

Field, S. (1990). *Trends in crime and their interpretation: A study of recorded crime in post-war England and Wales*, Home Office Research Study No. 119, HMSO, London.

Field, S. (1998). *Trends in crime revisited*, HMSO, London.

Graham, J. and Bowling, B. (1995). *Young People and Crime.* Home Office Research Study No.145. London, Home Office.

Hale, C. (1997). *The labour market and post-war crime trends in England & Wales.* Crime Unlimited: Questions for the 21st century. Macmillan, Basingstoke.

Hale, C. (1998). Crime and the business cycle in post-war Britain revisited. *British Journal of Criminology*, 38: 681-698.

Marvell, T. and Moody, C. (1996). Specification problems, police levels, and crime rates. *Criminology*, 34: 609-646.

Melliss, C (1997). *The Treasury forecasting record: An evaluation.* Discussion paper No. 47, ESRC Macroeconomic Modelling Bureau.

Mirrlees-Black, C., Budd, T., Partridge, S. and Mayhew, P. (1998). *The 1998 British Crime Survey.* Home Office Statistical Bulletin 21/98. London, Home Office.

Osborne, D. (1995). *Crime and the UK economy*, Robert Shuman Centre Working Paper 95/15, European University Institute.

Pudney, S., Pyle, D. and Deadman, D. (forthcoming). The relationship between crime, punishment and economic conditions. Is reliable inference possible when crimes are under-recorded? *Journal of the Royal Statistical Society, Series A.*

Pyle, D. and Deadman, D. (1994). Crime and the business cycle in post-war Britain. *British Journal of Criminology*, 34: 339-357.

Shaw, C. (1994). Accuracy and uncertainty of the national population projections for the United Kingdom. *Population Trends* 77: 24-32. HMSO, London.

Steffensmeier, D. and Harer, M. D. (1999). Making sense of recent US crime trends, 1980 to 1996/1998: Age composition and other explanations. *Journal of Research in Crime and Delinquency*, Vol. 36 No. 3: 235-274.

Witt, R., Clarke, A. and Fielding, N. (1999). Crime and Economic Activity: A Panel Data Approach. *British Journal of Criminology*, 39: 391-400.

Technical Annex

Time series properties of the data

Data for the period 1951 to 1998 were obtained from various editions of 'Criminal Statistics' and 'Economic Trends' and from the Office for National Statistics. In common with most economic time-series analysis, all data were expressed as logarithms. This has the effect of 'linearising' recorded crime and household consumption, both of which increase at a roughly constant rate over time. Table 1 summarises the time series analysed.

Table 1:   Data definitions

Time Series	Definition
Theft and handling stolen goods	Categories 37, 39-49 & 54 from Criminal Statistics
Burglary	Categories 28 to 31 from Criminal Statistics
Consumption	Total household final consumption expenditure (ABPF) at 1995 prices
Males aged 15	Mid-year population estimates
Males aged 20	Mid-year population estimates
Stock of goods	(Stock of goods)$_t$ = Consumption$_t$ + ... + Consumption$_{t-3}$
Young males	(Young males)$_t$ = (Males aged 15)$_t$ + (Males aged 20)$_t$

To compensate for changes in the counting rules for property crime in 1969[4] the burglary and theft time series for years up to and including 1969 were increased by 40 per cent and 2 per cent respectively. Also, because demographic data before 1961 are only available for five-year age groups (10-14, 15-19, etc.), the number of males aged 15 was set equal to the number aged 15-19 divided by five for these years. Similarly, the number of males aged 20 was set equal to the number aged 20-24 divided by five.

The order of integration of the data was determined using the Augmented Dickey-Fuller (ADF) test. This is based on constructing a regression model of the hypothesised level of integration and then testing the significance of the coefficients. The basic Dickey-Fuller test does not include lagged values of the dependent variable as explanatory variables. However, doing so is usually

---

4   The Theft Act (1968) re-classified certain theft offences and introduced the offence of aggravated burglary.

helpful as a way of removing serial correlation in the test residuals – which is essential for interpreting the test results. The number of lagged values included is known as the level of augmentation. Results of the ADF test also depend on whether the test regression includes a trend and/or constant term.

Choosing the 'correct' ADF test from the wide range of possible parameter combinations is important because mis-specification reduces the power of the test, which can cause problems for any subsequent analysis. For example, Pyle and Deadman (1994, 1997) report that crime series are I(2) and so analyse their data after twice differencing it. By contrast, Osborne (1995), Hale (1998) and Field (1998) all conclude that crime series are I(1). Osborne and Hale both make the convincing argument that Pyle and Deadman's analysis was flawed because it arbitrarily set the level of augmentation to one and failed to include a constant term when testing the null hypothesis of an I(2) process against an I(1) alternative.

The procedure for testing each variable was to carry out three 'blocks' of four tests. Each block covered different determinate variable combinations (no constant/no trend; constant only; constant and trend) and within each block different levels of augmentation (from zero to three) were tested.

Attention was focussed mainly on the third block of tests (those which included a constant and trend term) unless there was reason to suspect that the data were not time trended. The test results were themselves tested for serial correlation – where this was detected the corresponding ADF statistic was ignored. In some cases the null hypothesis was both rejected and not rejected depending on the level of augmentation. Where this occurred the test statistic with the lowest level of augmentation was chosen. Test results are shown in Tables 2 to 6 below.

Table 2: Augmented Dickey-Fuller Unit Root Test on Log(Theft and handling)

Exogenous variables	Lags	H_0: I(3) vs. H_1: I(2)		H_0 I(2) vs. H_1 I(1)		H_0 I(1) vs. H_1: I(0)	
		τ	Outcome	τ	Outcome	τ	Outcome
No constant/no trend	3	-5.7373	Reject ^	-1.9642	Reject	1.9484	Do not reject
No constant/no trend	2	-5.2856	Reject *	-2.1516	Reject	2.5771	Do not reject
No constant/no trend	1	-6.9951	Reject !	-3.1098	Reject	2.2257	Do not reject ^ !
No constant/no trend	0	-7.8965	Reject	-3.5001	Reject ^ !	3.6839	Do not reject **
Constant only	3	-5.7009	Reject ^	-2.8846	Do not reject	-2.9121	Do not reject
Constant only	2	-5.2257	Reject *	-3.1540	Reject	-2.8562	Do not reject ^ !
Constant only	1	-6.9079	Reject * !	-4.4012	Reject	-2.2396	Do not reject
Constant only	0	-7.8062	Reject	-4.4117	Reject ^ !	-1.6922	Do not reject*
Constant and trend	3	-5.6929	Reject ^	-4.1138	Reject	-0.8425	Do not reject
Constant and trend	2	-5.1604	Reject *	-4.2909	Reject	-0.7063	Do not reject ^
Constant and trend	1	-6.8989	Reject * !	-5.3666	Reject ^ !	-1.2161	Do not reject !
Constant and trend	0	-7.8250	Reject	-4.9191	Reject	0.1639	Do not reject *

*(**) indicates the presence of serial correlation at the 5%(1%) level
^ indicates the best model as judged by the Akaike Information Criterion
! indicates the best model as judged by the Schwarz Bayesian Criterion
Sample (unadjusted): 1951 1998
Tests calculated using Eviews 3.1

Table 3: Augmented Dickey-Fuller Unit Root Test on Log(Burglary)

Exogenous variables	Lags	H₀: I(3) vs. H₁: I(2)		H₀ I(2) vs. H₁ I(1)		H₀ I(1) vs. H₁: I(0)	
		τ	Outcome	τ	Outcome	τ	Outcome
No constant/no trend	3	-5.7832	Reject ^ !	-2.5455	Reject	1.9610	Do not reject
No constant/no trend	2	-4.9988	Reject *	-2.6621	Reject	2.1779	Do not reject
No constant/no trend	1	-6.7252	Reject	-3.5093	Reject	1.7688	Do not reject ^ !
No constant/no trend	0	-8.5800	Reject	-3.9834	Reject ^ !	2.7159	Do not reject*
Constant only	3	-5.7474	Reject ^ !	-3.4866	Reject	-2.9603	Reject
Constant only	2	-4.9366	Reject *	-3.5946	Reject	-2.6975	Do not reject ^ !
Constant only	1	-6.6418	Reject	-4.4506	Reject ^	-1.9721	Do not reject*
Constant only	0	-8.4811	Reject	-4.5577	Reject!	-1.4798	Do not reject*
Constant and trend	3	-5.6600	Reject ^ !	-4.3890	Reject	-2.1102	Do not reject
Constant and trend	2	-4.8751	Reject *	-4.4393	Reject	-1.9036	Do not reject ^ !
Constant and trend	1	-6.6835	Reject	-5.0681	Reject ^ !	-1.9520	Do not reject *
Constant and trend	0	-8.5275	Reject	-4.8305	Reject	-0.6880	Do not reject *

*(*) indicates the presence of serial correlation at the 5%(1%) level
^ indicates the best model as judged by the Akaike Information Criterion
! indicates the best model as judged by the Schwarz Bayesian Criterion
Sample (unadjusted): 1951 1998
Tests calculated using Eviews 3.1

Table 4: Augmented Dickey-Fuller Unit Root Test on Log(Consumption)

Exogenous variables	Lags	H_0: I(3) vs. H_1: I(2)		H_0 I(2) vs. H_1 I(1)		H_0 I(1) vs. H_1: I(0)	
		τ	Outcome	τ	Outcome	τ	Outcome
No constant/no trend	3	-5.6278	Reject ^	-1.3891	Do not reject	3.7491	Do not reject
No constant/no trend	2	-5.3942	Reject	-1.9334	Do not reject	3.9178	Do not reject ^
No constant/no trend	1	-6.3440	Reject*	-2.4329	Reject	3.3413	Do not reject!
No constant/no trend	0	-7.2980	Reject !	-2.5716	Reject ^ !	8.3962	Do not reject **
Constant only	3	-5.5511	Reject ^	-4.1181	Reject	-0.1142	Do not reject
Constant only	2	-5.3216	Reject	-4.3724	Reject	-0.2452	Do not reject ^
Constant only	1	-6.2674	Reject*	-4.8438	Reject ^	-0.2974	Do not reject !
Constant only	0	-7.2135	Reject !	-4.4089	Reject !	-0.5286	Do not reject **
Constant and trend	3	-5.4759	Reject ^	-4.0750	Reject	-2.7283	Do not reject
Constant and trend	2	-5.2321	Reject	-4.3000	Reject	-2.9845	Do not reject
Constant and trend	1	-6.2035	Reject*	-4.7772	Reject ^	-3.7422	Reject ^ !
Constant and trend	0	-7.1326	Reject !	-4.3514	Reject !	-2.3722	Do not reject **

*(**) indicates the presence of serial correlation at the 5%(1%) level
^ indicates the best model as judged by the Akaike Information Criterion
! indicates the best model as judged by the Schwarz Bayesian Criterion
Sample (unadjusted): 1951 1998
Tests calculated using Eviews 3.1

Table 5: Augmented Dickey-Fuller Unit Root Test on Log(Young males)

Exogenous variables	Lags	H_0: I(3) vs. H_1: I(2)		H_0 I(2) vs. H_1 I(1)		H_0 I(1) vs. H_1: I(0)	
		τ	Outcome	τ	Outcome	τ	Outcome
No constant/no trend	3	-6.7173	Reject ^ !	-2.3383	Reject *	0.3972	Do not reject
No constant/no trend	2	-6.2953	Reject *	-3.1205	Reject	0.4347	Do not reject
No constant/no trend	1	-6.7564	Reject **	-3.6546	Reject	0.4249	Do not reject ^
No constant/no trend	0	-9.7914	Reject *	-4.9009	Reject ^ !	0.6423	Do not reject !
Constant only	3	-6.6285	Reject ^ !	-2.3355	Do not reject *	-2.0191	Do not reject
Constant only	2	-6.2135	Reject*	-3.1152	Reject	-2.0215	Do not reject
Constant only	1	-6.6728	Reject **	-3.6480	Reject	-1.8308	Do not reject ^
Constant only	0	-9.6749	Reject *	-4.8760	Reject ^ !	-1.7765	Do not reject !
Constant and trend	3	-6.5399	Reject ^ !	-3.3337	Do not reject	-0.8670	Do not reject
Constant and trend	2	-6.1336	Reject *	-4.0085	Reject	-0.9562	Do not reject
Constant and trend	1	-6.5848	Reject **	-4.3873	Reject	-0.8591	Do not reject
Constant and trend	0	-9.5590	Reject *	-5.4334	Reject ^ !	-0.4641	Do not reject ^ !

*(**) indicates the presence of serial correlation at the 5%(1%) level
^ indicates the best model as judged by the Akaike Information Criterion
! indicates the best model as judged by the Schwarz Bayesian Criterion
Sample (unadjusted): 1951 1998
Tests calculated using Eviews 3.1

Table 6: Augmented Dickey-Fuller Unit Root Test on Log(Stock of goods)

Exogenous variables	Lags	H_0: I(3) vs. H_1: I(2)		H_0 I(2) vs. H_1 I(1)		H_0 I(1) vs. H_1: I(0)	
		τ	Outcome	τ	Outcome	τ	Outcome
No constant/no trend	3	-5.9444	Reject ^ !	-0.9416	Do not reject *	3.9398	Do not reject
No constant/no trend	2	-4.6747	Reject *	-1.3573	Do not reject ^	4.3109	Do not reject ^ !
No constant/no trend	1	-4.5972	Reject	-1.5539	Do not reject !	2.3866	Do not reject **
No constant/no trend	0	-4.1771	Reject	-0.8114	Do not reject**	13.9198	Do not reject**
Constant only	3	-5.8624	Reject ^ !	-3.6925	Reject	-0.0098	Do not reject
Constant only	2	-4.6143	Reject *	-4.2568	Reject	-0.3653	Do not reject ^ !
Constant only	1	-4.5343	Reject	-4.7275	Reject ^ !	-0.5587	Do not reject **
Constant only	0	-4.1292	Reject	-2.5541	Do not reject **	-0.0904	Do not reject **
Constant and trend	3	-5.8086	Reject ^ !	-3.6433	Reject	-2.3049	Do not reject
Constant and trend	2	-4.5513	Reject *	-4.1873	Reject	-2.5879	Do not reject ^ !
Constant and trend	1	-4.4693	Reject	-4.6766	Reject ^ !	-5.0971	Reject *
Constant and trend	0	-4.0784	Reject	-2.5283	Do not reject **	-1.5280	Do not reject **

*(**) indicates the presence of serial correlation at the 5%(1%) level
^ indicates the best model as judged by the Akaike Information Criterion
! indicates the best model as judged by the Schwarz Bayesian Criterion
Sample (unadjusted): 1951 1998
Tests calculated using Eviews 3.1

All the variables were found to be I(1) with the exception of Log(Consumption), which was found to be I(0). The consumption result is counter-intuitive and further examination revealed that the I(1) test was only marginally rejected. On this basis, the variable was treated as I(1). To successfully model the relationship among I(1) variables it is necessary to establish that they are 'cointegrated'.[5] Failure to do so raises the possibility that any relationship among the variables is 'spurious'.[6]

Models of theft and handling and burglary

Regressions with cointegrating variables can be parameterised in a number of ways, but a particularly informative approach is to split the equation into an error-correction mechanism, which represents the deviation from the long-run equilibrium, with the remaining variables representing dynamic short-run changes. For example, suppose the following relationship holds:

$$y_t = \alpha_0 + \alpha_1 y_{t-1} + \alpha_2 y_{t-2} + \alpha_3 x_t + \alpha_4 x_{t-1} + \alpha_5 x_{t-2} + \varepsilon_t \qquad\qquad \varepsilon_t \sim N(0, \sigma^2) \qquad (1)$$

where x_t and y_t are cointegrated with $y_t = \lambda x_t$. This can be re-written as:

$$\Delta y_t = \beta_0 + \beta_1 (y_{t-1} - \lambda x_{t-1}) + \beta_2 \Delta y_{t-1} + \beta_3 \Delta x_{t-1} + \varepsilon_t \qquad (2)$$

where the second term on the right-hand side is the error-correction mechanism. Note that the sign of the associated coefficient, β_1, should be negative – a positive coefficient would reinforce any deviation from the long-run equilibrium.

The Engle-Granger procedure was used to test for cointegration: first the un-differenced dependent variable (either burglary or theft and handling) was regressed on the un-differenced explanatory variables (stock of goods and number of young males). Then the residuals from this regression were tested to see if they contained a unit root, using an ADF test with modified critical values. Results are shown in Tables 7 to 10 below.

---

5   Banerjee *et al.* (1993) define cointegration as follows: "The components of the vector x_t are said to be cointegrated of order d, b, denoted $x_t \sim \text{CI(d,b)}$, if (i) x_t is I(d) and (ii) there exists a non-zero vector α such that $\alpha.x_t \sim \text{I(d-b)}$, d $\geq$ b > 0." In this case we are looking for a linear combination of I(1) variables that is I(0).

6   Banerjee *et al.* (1993) define a spurious regression as "regression of an integrated series on another unrelated integrated series [that] produces *t*-ratios on the slope parameter which indicate a relationship much more often than they should at the nominal test level." They go on to point out that "the problem will not disappear as the sample size is increased."

Table 7: **Long-run model for theft and handling stolen goods**

Sample: 1951 – 1998 (48 observations)
Standard errors & t-statistics in parentheses

Log(Theft and handling) = *1.719* Log(Stock of goods) +*1.078* Log(Young males) - *29.007*

	(0.044)	(0.113)	(1.318)
	(39.096)	(9.509)	(-22.006)

R-squared	0.984	Mean dependent variable	9.281
Adjusted R-squared	0.983	S.D. dependent variable	0.691
S.E. equation	0.090	Akaike Info Criterion	-1.917
Sum sq. resids	0.365	Schwarz Bayesian Criterion	-1.800
Log likelihood	49.001	F-statistic	1,359.928

Table 8: **Unit root test for residuals of the long-run theft and handling equation**

	Test Statistic	Maximised log-likelihood	Akaike Information Criterion	Schwarz Bayesian Criterion	Hannan-Quinn Criterion
DF	-2.6915	56.7027	55.7027	54.8221	55.3779
ADF(1)	-4.3660	62.5359	60.5359	58.7747	59.8864
ADF(2)	-3.9935	62.9424	59.9424	57.3006	58.9682
ADF(3)	-4.2765	64.4641	60.4641	56.9417	59.1652

95 per cent critical value for the modified Dickey-Fuller statistic = -3.9444

Note: The ADF(1) statistic is the preferred test statistic according to the Akaike Information Criterion, Schwarz Bayesian Criterion and Hannan-Quinn Criterion.

Table 9: **Long-run model for burglary**

Sample: 1951 – 1998 (48 observations)
Standard errors & t-statistics in parentheses

Log(Burglary) =	*1.875* Log(Stock of goods)	+*1.221* Log(Young males)	*-33.933*
	(0.065)	(0.168)	(1.956)
	(28.721)	(7.258)	(-17.344)

R-squared	0.971	Mean dependent variable	8.431
Adjusted R-squared	0.969	S.D. dependent variable	0.762
S.E. equation	0.134	Akaik Info Criterion	-1.127
Sum sq. resids	0.804	Schwarz Bayesian Criterion	-1.010
Log likelihood	30.044	F-statistic	742.038

Table 10: Unit root test for residuals of the long-run burglary equation

	Test Statistic	Maximised log-likelihood	Akaike Information Criterion	Schwarz Bayesian Criterion	Hannan-Quinn Criterion
DF	-3.0150	41.3289	40.3289	39.4483	40.0042
ADF(1)	-4.1504	45.4104	43.4104	41.6492	42.7609
ADF(2)	-4.1308	46.0908	43.0908	40.4490	42.1166
ADF(3)	-4.3780	47.4079	43.4079	39.8855	42.1090

95 per cent critical value for the modified Dickey-Fuller statistic = -3.9444

Note: The ADF(1) test statistic is the preferred test statistic according to the Akaike Information Criterion, Schwarz Bayesian Criterion and Hannan-Quinn Criterion.

For both models the preferred test statistic is larger than the critical value, indicating that the residuals are I(0), and therefore that the variables in the two regression models are indeed cointegrated. Having established cointegration, it is usual to estimate the full ECM by substituting the residuals from the Engle-Granger procedure into the $(y_t - \lambda x_t)$ term in Equation 2 above:

$$\Delta y_t = \beta_0 + \beta_1 (\text{Engle-Granger residuals})_{t-1} + \beta_2 \Delta y_{t-1} + \beta_3 \Delta x_{t-1} + \varepsilon_t \qquad (3)$$

However, this approach has been criticised because of the effect of small sample bias on the parameter estimates. It is better to specify the model as a full 'dynamic' model. This involves expanding out Equation 2 as follows:

$$\Delta y_t = \delta_0 + \delta_1 y_{t-1} + \delta_2 x_{t-1} + \delta_3 \Delta y_{t-1} + \delta_4 \Delta x_{t-1} + \varepsilon_t \qquad (4)$$

This produces an equation that is I(0) on the left-hand side but has two I(1) variables on the right-hand side. However, this does not invalidate the approach since we have already established cointegration[7]. The full dynamic models are detailed in Tables 11 and 12 below.

---

7   This is essentially the approach taken by Hale (1998). Note that it does not address the issue of pre-test bias.

Table 11: Full dynamic model for theft and handling stolen goods

Sample: 1952 – 1998 (47 observations)
Standard errors & t-statistics in parentheses

ΔLog(Theft and handling)$_t$ =

$- 0.383$ Log(Theft and handling)$_{t-1}$	$+ 0.634$ Log(Stock of goods)$_{t-1}$
(0.088)	(0.157)
(-4.368)	(4.027)
$+ 0.468$ Log(Young Males)$_{t-1}$	$- 1.413$ ΔLog(Consumption)$_t$
(0.103)	(0.333)
(4.569)	(-4.243)
$+ 0.792$ ΔLog(Consumption)$_{t-1}$	$+ 0.500$ ΔLog(Theft and handling)$_{t-1}$ $- 12.371$
(0.390)	(0.109) (2.771)
(2.032)	(4.597) (-4.465)

R-squared	0.698	Mean dependent variable	0.037
Adjusted R-squared	0.652	S.D. dependent variable	0.068
S.E. equation	0.040	Akaike Info Criterion	-3.445
Sum sq. resids	0.065	Schwarz Bayesian Criterion	-3.170
Log likelihood	87.96	F-statistic	15.386

Table 12: Full dynamic model for burglary

Sample: 1952 – 1998 (47 observations)
Standard errors & t-statistics in parentheses

ΔLog(Burglary)$_t$ =

$- 0.317$ Log(Burglary)$_{t-1}$	$+ 0.545$ Log(Stock of goods)$_{t-1}$	$+ 0.478$ Log(Young Males)$_{t-1}$
(0.084)	(0.168)	(0.121)
(-3.794)	(3.238)	(3.960)
$- 2.088$ ΔLog(Consumption)$_t$	$+ 0.364$ ΔLog(Burglary)$_{t-1}$	$- 11.944$
(0.494)	(0.108)	(3.080)
(-4.228)	(3.369)	(-3.878)

R-squared	0.631	Mean dependent variable	0.042
Adjusted R-squared	0.586	S.D. dependent variable	0.099
S.E. equation	0.064	Akaike Info Criterion	-2.556
Sum sq. resids	0.166	Schwarz Bayesian Criterion	-2.319
Log likelihood	66.055	F-statistic	14.047

Specification tests

Note that both models include $\Delta Log(Consumption)_t$ as an additional exogenous variable. This is valid since it does not unbalance the equations – however it is important to check that $\Delta Log(Consumption)_t$ is not contemporaneously correlated with the error term. This was done using the Wu-Hausman test and the results, along with other standard specification tests, are reported in Table 13 below.

Table 13: Standard specification tests

Tests (calculated using Eviews 3.1)	p-value	
	Theft and handling	Burglary
Normality of residuals (Jarque-Bera)	0.889	0.944
Serial correlation in residuals (Breusch-Godfrey with 2 lags):		
F test version	0.999	0.185
LM test version	1.000	0.143
Heteroscedasticity in residuals (White):		
F test version (with no cross terms)	0.478	0.834
Asymptotic test version (with no cross terms)	0.432	0.786
F test version (with cross terms)	0.421	0.877
Asymptotic test version (with cross terms)	0.377	0.784
Auto-regressive conditional heteroscedasticity in residuals (with 1 lag):		
F test version	0.153	0.876
Asymptotic test version	0.147	0.873
Non-linearity of model (Ramsey with 3 fitted terms):		
F test version	0.941	0.437
Asymptotic test version	0.920	0.345
Exogeneity of non-lagged consumption variable (Wu-Hausman):		
F test version	0.913	0.547
Asymptotic test version	0.903	0.510

In addition to the standard tests, parameter stability was examined via the CUSUM and CUSUM of Squares tests. Results are shown in Figures 1 and 2 below. These suggest that, while the burglary model is reasonably stable, the theft and handling model may exhibit instability in the early 1970s and mid-1990s.

Figure 1a: **CUSUM test for the full dynamic model of theft and handling**

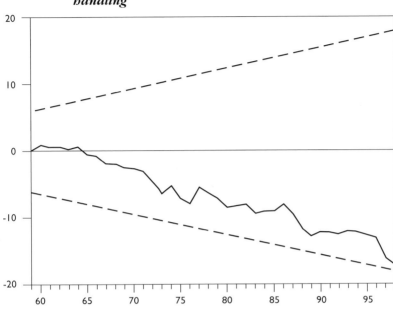

Figure 1b: **CUSUM of squares test for the full dynamic model of theft and handling**

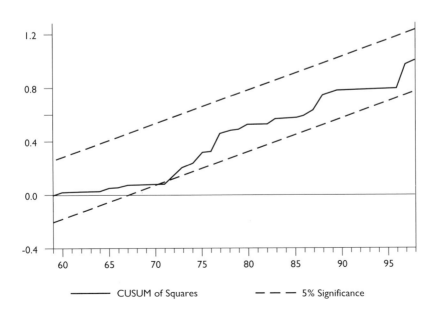

Figure 2a: CUSUM test for the full dynamic model of burglary

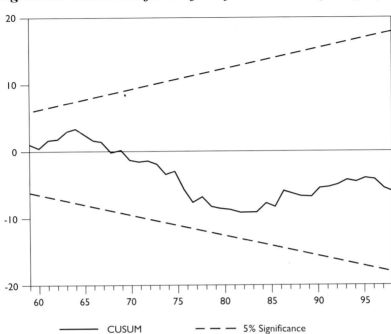

Figure 2b: CUSUM of squares test for the full dynamic model of burglary

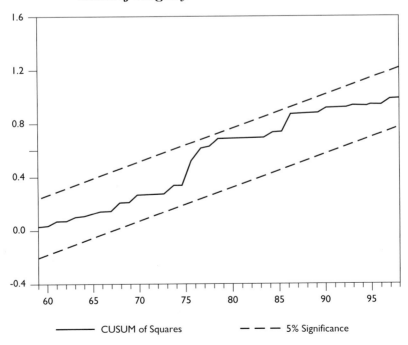

The instability in the model of theft and handling was examined further by plotting an n-step forecast test (essentially a graphical representation of a series of Chow forecast tests). The test, shown in Figure 3 below, highlights those years where actual levels of theft using the coefficients calculated on the sample up to that year would have been significantly different from forecast theft. The dots below the residual plot show where the model is least successful – those points where the model up to that year cannot satisfactorily explain the level of theft after that year (the p-value of the test for each year is given on the left vertical axis of the graph).

Figure 3: N-step forecast test for the full dynamic model of theft and handling

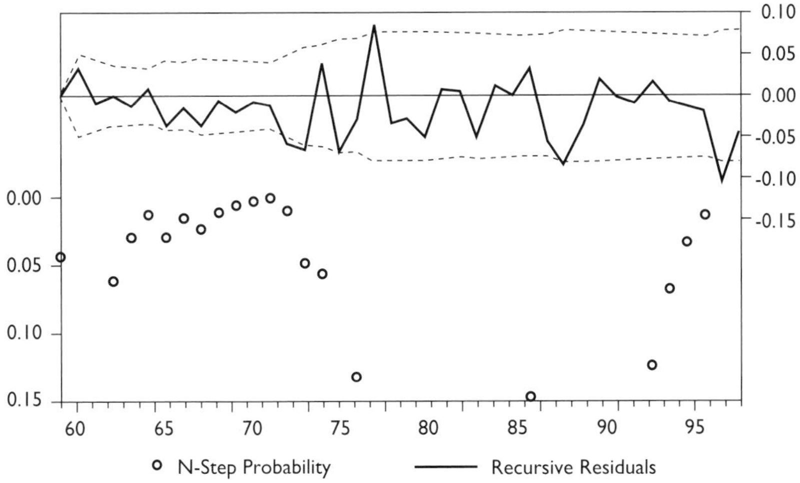

The structural breaks in the early 1970s could be the result of changes to the recording rules for crime in 1969, although both recorded crime time series were adjusted to correct for these changes. It is possible that theft and handling was more profoundly affected by the changes because it covers a more disparate group of offences. It is hard to find a reason for the mid-1990s structural break.

Projections

Projections were made using the two full dynamic models in conjunction with Treasury forecasts for household consumption and GAD forecasts of population levels. The projections for 1999 were based on actual recorded crime for 1998. Projections for subsequent years were based on projected crime levels in the preceding year. The results are shown in Figures 5 and 6 in the main text.

The projections are subject to four potential sources of error:

- Specification error: Parameter instability in the model of theft and handling indicates that these projections should be treated with caution. Other factors, such as the Crime Reduction Programme might also significantly change the structure of the two models.

- Conditioning error: Any errors in the Treasury and GAD forecasts will be directly incorporated into these projections.

- Sampling error: The parameter estimates are based on the sample period 1951 to 1998 and will not be the same as the 'true' parameter values.

- Random error: The predictions assume the error terms ε_{1998+i} all equal zero.

Parameter stability

To further test the sensitivity of this model a number of projections were made using variations of the basic model that exclude data from the early 1950s. The results in Table 16 below provide more evidence of instability in the theft and handling model.[8]

Table 16: Projection instability in the theft and handling model

Sample period	Central projection for 2001
1952 – 98	3.29 million
1953 – 98	3.07 million
1954 – 98	3.01 million
1955 – 98	2.88 million
1956 – 98	2.89 million
1957 – 98	2.89 million
1958 – 98	2.90 million
1959 – 98	2.85 million
1960 – 98	2.79 million

One way to test the possibility that the data in the years 1952 to 1954 are unrepresentative of the sample as a whole, and thus are causing instability in the model, is to run a series of regressions, sequentially removing the most distant year, and inspecting the resulting parameter estimates. If these estimates shift significantly, it suggests there may be structural instability in a model that includes the earlier years.

---

8   The projections shown here are unconstrained by actual recorded crime figures, and so are not directly comparable to the projections in Table 1 in the text.

An inspection of these 'recursive coefficients' for the theft model from the full 1952-1998 model through to the 1960-1998 model revealed small shifts in some of the parameters of the model, but these were insignificant. On balance, there does not seem enough evidence to justify censoring the data set by removing the earlier years from the analysis. Put another way, the model is not obviously improved by removing these years. Therefore both models were run on the full time period available given the data: 1951 to 1998.

One issue that may be of relevance here is the quality of the young males data in the 1950s. As stated above, the data between 1951 and 1960 are only available in five-year age groups. This may have the effect of distorting any relationship between the single year groups and the crime variables over the period.

Choice of demographic variable

The main criteria for choosing an appropriate demographic variable are that the variable should:

• have some statistical basis in criminological theory (eg. peak age of offending);

• be $I(1)$;

• be cointegrated with the crime and stock variables;

• provide the highest information level in a model (according to the Akaike Information Criteria and Schwarz Bayesian Criteria); or

• result in the most 'stable' model (according to CUSUM or similar test).

The young males variable used in Field (1998) was constructed as the number of males aged 15 plus the number of males aged 20. Whilst this formulation is $I(1)$ and cointegrated with the other long-run variables, it has no clear grounding in theory – as Field says, the variable is "somewhat artificial". Further work was therefore carried out to test other, more suitable young males variables for possible inclusion in the model.

Two sources of information were used to construct a list of theoretically sound variables. The first was data on the age distribution of the number of young males cautioned and found guilty of theft and burglary offences ("known offending"). The second was a study by Graham and Bowling (1995) which used a survey approach to investigating relationships between young people and crime.

A number of variables were considered. The level of integration of these variables was tested, and those found to be I(1) were retained. The following variables were shortlisted:

Table 17: Possible alternative young males variables

Theoretical justification	Variable
The peak age of known male offending for burglary	Males aged 17
The peak age of known male offending for theft	Males aged 17
The smallest age range covering one quarter of all known male burglary offenders	Males 16 to 18
The smallest age range covering one fifth of all known male theft offenders	Males 16 to 18
The peak age of surveyed male property offending	Males aged 20

These variables were then tested in the burglary and theft models in place of the existing 'Males aged 15 plus males aged 20' variable. The results were mixed. In general, the new demographic variables entered the models at the cost of reduced information (according to the Akaike Information Criteria and Schwarz Bayesian Criteria). However, there were significant differences between the burglary and theft models.

The burglary model was only marginally affected by the introduction of a new variable. The variable that caused the least loss of information in comparison with the existing variable was 'Males aged 16 to 18'. The theft model was considerably more sensitive to the inclusion of alternate young males variables. This model already exhibits a number of problems, notably parameter instability and failure of the n-step forecast test, and these new demographic variables created more severe problems in these areas. It was therefore decided to retain the original 'Males aged 15 and males aged 20' variable used by Field.

Publications

List of research publications

The most recent research reports published are listed below. A **full** list of publications is available on request from the Research, Development and Statistics Directorate, Information and Publications Group.

Home Office Research Studies (HORS)

189. **Mandatory drug testing in prisons: The relationship between MDT and the level and nature of drug misuse**. Kimmett Edgar and Ian O'Donnell. 1998

190. **Trespass and protest: policing under the Criminal Justice and Public Order Act 1994**. Tom Bucke and Zoë James. 1998.

191. **Domestic Violence: Findings from a new British Crime Survey self-completion questionnaire.** Catriona Mirrlees-Black. 1999.

192. **Explaining reconviction following a community sentence: the role of social factors.** Chris May. 1999.

193. **Domestic Violence Matters: an evaluation of a development project**. Liz Kelly. 1999.

194. **Increasing confidence in community sentences: the results of two demonstration projects**. Carol Hedderman, Tom Ellis and Darren Sugg. 1999.

195. **Trends in Crime Revisted.** Simon Field. 1999.

196. **A question of evidence? Investigating and prosecuting rape in the 1990s**. Jessica Harris and Sharon Grace. 1999.

197. **Drug Misuse Declared in 1998: results from the British Crime Survey**. Malcolm Ramsay and Sarah Partridge. 1999.

Research Findings

70. **Drug testing arrestees.** Trevor Bennett. 1998.

71. **Prevention of plastic card fraud.** Michael Levi and Jim Handley. 1998.

72. **Offending on bail and police use of conditional bail.** David Brown. 1998.

73. **Voluntary after-care.** Mike Maguire, Peter Raynor, Maurice Vanstone and Jocelyn Kynch. 1998.

74. **Fast-tracking of persistent young offenders.** John Graham. 1998.

75. **Mandatory drug testing in prisons – an evaluation.** Kimmett Edgar and Ian O'Donnell. 1998.

76. **The prison population in 1997: a statistical review.** Philip White. 1998.

77. **Rural areas and crime: findings from the British crime survey.** Catriona Mirrlees-Black. 1998.

78. **A review of classification systems for sex offenders.** Dawn Fisher and George Mair. 1998.

79. **An evaluation of the prison sex offender treatment programme.** Anthony Beech et al. 1998.

80. **Age limits for babies in prison: some lessons from abroad.** Diane Caddle. 1998.

81. **Motor projects in England & Wales: an evaluation.** Darren Sugg. 1998

82. **HIV/Aids risk behaviour among adult male prisoners.** John Strange et al. 1998.

83. **Concern about crime: findings from the 1998 British Crime Survey.** Catriona Mirrlees-Black and Jonathan Allen. 1998.

84. **Transfers from prison to hospital - the operation of section 48 of the Mental Health Act 1983.** Ronnie Mackay and David Machin. 1998.

85. **Evolving crack cocaine careers.** Kevin Brain, Howard Parker and Tim Bottomley. 1998.

86. **Domestic Violence: Findings from the BCS self-completion questionnaire.** 1999. Catriona Mirrlees-Black and Carole Byron. 1999.

87. **Incentives and earned privileges for prisoners – an evaluation.** Alison Liebling, Grant Muir, Gerry Rose and Anthony Bottoms. 1999.

88. **World Prison Population List.** Roy Walmsley. 1999.

89. **Probation employment schemes in inner London and Surrey – an evaluation.** Chris Samo, Michael Hough, Claire Nee and Victoria Herrington. 1999.

90. **Reconviction of offenders sentenced or released from prison in 1994.** Chris Kershaw. 1999.

91. **Domestic violence matters: an evaluation of a development project.** Liz Kelly. 1999.

92. **Increasing confidence in community sentences.** Carol Hedderman, Tom Ellis and Darren Sugg. 1999.

94. **The Prison Population in 1998: a statistical review.** Philip White. 1999.

95. **Using Mentors to Change Problem Behaviour in Primary School Children.** Ian St James Roberts and Clifford Samial Singh. 1999.

96. **Meeting Need and Challenging Crime in Partnership with Schools.** Graham Vulliamy and Rosemary Webb. 1999.

97. **The role of social factors in predicting reconviction for offenders on community penalties.** Chris May. 1999.

98. **Community penalties for fine default and persistent petty offending.** Robin Elliott, Jennifer Airs and Stefan Webb. 1999.

99. **Demanding physical activity programmes for young offenders.** Peter Taylor, Iain Crow, Dominic Irvine and Geoff Nichols. 1999.

100. **The admissibility and sufficiency of evidence in child abuse prosecutions.** Gwynn Davis, Laura Hoyano, Caroline Keenan, Lee Maitland and Rod Morgan. 1999.

101. **Reconviction of offenders sentenced or released from prison in 1995.** Chris Kershaw, Joanne Goodman and Steve White. 1999.

Occasional Papers

Monitoring and evaluation of WOLDS remand prison and comparisons with public-sector prisons, in particular HMP Woodhill. A Keith Bottomley, Adrian James, Emma Clare and Alison Liebling. 1997.

Evaluation of the 'One Stop Shop' and victim statement pilot projects. Carolyn Hoyle, Ed Cape, Rod Morgan and Andrew Sanders. 1998.

Restorative Justice: an overview. Tony Marshall. 1999.

Step 3: an evaluation of the prison sex offender treatment programme. Anthony Beech, Dawn Fisher and Richard Beckett. 1999.

The Impact of the National Lottery on the Horserace Betting Levy: Fourth Report. Sam Brand. 1999.

An assessment of the admissibility and sufficiency of evidence in child abuse prosecutions. Gwynn Davis, Laura Hoyano, Caroline Keenan, Lee Maitland and Rod Morgan. 1999.

Violence at work: findings from the British Crime Survey. Tracey Budd. 1999.

Demanding physical activity programmes for young offenders under probation supervision. Peter Taylor, Iain Crow, Dominic Irvine and Geoff Nichols. 1999.

Requests for Publications

Home Office Research Studies, Research Findings and *Occasional Papers* can be requested from:

Research, Development and Statistics Directorate
Information and Publications Group
Room 201, Home Office
50 Queen Anne's Gate
London SW1H 9AT
Telephone: 020 7273 2084
Facsimile: 020 7222 0211
Internet: http://www.homeoffice.gov.uk/rds/index.htm
E-mail: rds.ho@gtnet.gov.uk